Getting
What You
Want

Also by Jerry Minchinton

Maximum Self-Esteem

*52 Things You Can Do to
Raise Your Self-Esteem*

Wising Up

Thinking Better

Getting What You Want

The 10 Steps
to Reaching
Your Goals

Jerry Minchinton

arnford house

Library of Congress Control Number: 2005902666

Minchinton, Jerry.

Getting what you want : the 10 steps to reaching your goals /
Jerry Minchinton. -- Vanzant, MO : Arnford House, 2005.

p. ; cm.

A fable within a story, the book describes the ten steps
necessary to reach any goal.

.ISBN: 09635719-2-3
1. Goal (Psychology) 2. Motivation (Psychology)
3. Self-actualization (Psychology) 4. Success--
   Psychological aspects.

I. Title.

BF505.G6 M56 2005 2005902666

153.8--dc22 0509

Printed in the United States of America
10 9 8 7 6 5 4 3 2 1

Arnford House is a division of the Arnford Corporation

Contents

The Class Reunion

Part 1

Bill Carson wondered what kind of an evening he had let himself in for when he decided to attend his high school class's 15-year reunion. Would he even know anybody there? *There is only one way to find out,* he decided.

He walked to the door of the gym where the party was being held, received his name tag, and went inside. The gym, criss-crossed with streamers, looked very much like it had when they'd held dances there in his school days but with the addition of a sign welcoming the returning senior class.

He saw a familiar face at the punch bowl. "Mr. Brown, how are you doing?" he asked one of his former teachers.

"Bill, you've been out of school long enough to call me Tom."

"It's good to see you again, Tom. I always enjoyed your classes."

"That's probably why I remember you so well. You were one of my best students."

Turning his eyes to the crowd again, Bill spotted a very familiar face.

"Tom, please excuse me. I just saw Alan Waters, my best friend in high school."

He walked over to Alan, and the two men shook hands.

"It's great to see you again, Bill," Alan said.

"You, too," Bill replied warmly. "Did you bring your wife?"

"I was married for a couple of years," Alan said, "but she divorced me. She said I didn't have any future. You probably remember her, Connie Owen, the class president?"

"I do remember her," Bill responded. "She was quite a pretty girl and very popular."

"How about you?" Alan said. "Did you get married?"

"Yes, I did," Bill said. "My wife wanted to be here tonight, but she had a family obligation she couldn't avoid."

"But what about you, Alan? What have you been doing?"

"Oh," Alan answered, "I haven't done too well. Just got a lot of bad breaks, I guess. Nothing ever seemed to work out for me."

"That's too bad," Bill said. "You had so many ambitious ideas and dreams. That's why the class voted you the most likely to succeed."

"Yes," Alan added, "I did have lots of dreams. I tried a number of different jobs. If I didn't see much chance for advancement in one, I'd move on to another and then another, trying to find a situation that really suited me. I was just living from day to day, waiting for my big break.

"Well, my break never happened, so for the past few years I've held a dishwashing job at one of the local restaurants. In fact, I've been so short of cash lately I didn't know if I'd be able to come to the reunion. My folks knew it was important to me, though, so they took care of my expenses."

"It looks like you've been lucky," Alan said, taking in Bill's hand-tailored suit and expensive Italian loafers. "Who died and left you a couple of million?"

"Nobody," Bill replied. "I did it the hard way, by starting a business and earning the millions myself. I haven't done too badly."

"If you don't owe your success to luck, what do you owe it to?" Alan asked.

"Remember Fred Decatur, the old man who lived down the street from me, the one you thought was a little out of touch with reality? I delivered papers to him and got to know him while I was going to high school. He was a lot smarter than people gave him credit for."

"What do you mean?" Alan asked.

"Well, when he died he had more than five million dollars in the bank."

"Wow!" Alan exclaimed. "He left his money to you!"

"He didn't leave me a penny. In fact, his entire estate went to charity. No, he left me something much better than money."

"What do you mean?" Alan asked.

"He told me a story to illustrate some important ideas, ideas that helped me become a success in every area of my life," Bill answered.

"That must be quite a story," Alan said. "How about sharing it with me?"

"Well," Bill responded, "you asked what I owe my success to, and you also want to know about the story he told me. Let me tell you the tale, and it will answer both of your questions. Let's find some place to sit down away from this crowd."

The two men walked outside into the summer evening, found a bench and sat down. Bill began his story.

The Story of the
Stolen Princess

King Bruno Offers
a Reward

All was not well in the kingdom of Giocoso. King Bruno's beloved daughter Melisande had been spirited away by the evil wizard Monstroso, and was being held captive in his Tower of Ice in the country of Malfeaso.

People were reluctant to try to rescue her because the wizard's country always looked terribly cold. Anyone going there would have to take special clothing and face freezing temperatures, blizzards, snow, and ice.

Monstroso said he would return the princess only if King Bruno paid him a huge ransom. If the king didn't pay within a year, Monstroso threatened to put a spell on Melisande that would make her so ugly that no one could stand to be around her.

King Bruno loved his daughter so much that he would willingly have paid Monstroso if the wizard had asked for a reasonable sum, but he had not. His demands far exceeded the King's ability to pay. To do what Monstroso asked the king would have to increase everyone's taxes for years to come, and this he would not do.

Since he couldn't pay the ransom, King Bruno came up with another idea. For some time he had been looking for a suitable husband for the princess, so he decided to offer his daughter's hand in marriage to the man who could overpower Monstroso and bring Melisande back safely. This was a very desirable reward, for not only was Melisande both beautiful and wise, whoever married her would become the next king of Giocoso.

The king sent word out to kingdoms and countries far and near, and would-be-rescuers arrived by the dozens. But as month after month passed and the Monstroso's deadline drew near, all those who had tried to find her admitted defeat. Some said they couldn't find the wizard's tower. Others felt there were too many obstacles to overcome, and some never returned at all. What was the king to do?

Noway and Kandu Arrive in Giocoso

The king began feeling a little more optimistic one bright spring morning when he was told that two men had arrived at the palace and wanted to speak with him. The first man was Noway, the Crown Prince of Aber, who had

just ridden into Giocoso. He had heard about the princess and the reward being offered, and having nothing better to do, thought he might as well have a try at finding her.

The other man was Kandu, an enterprising young archer from Schnell. Ever since he heard about the princess being kidnapped and the

reward King Bruno had promised, he had made rescuing her his most important goal.

As it turned out, Noway and Kandu arrived at the palace at the same time. When they were ushered into the throne room, King Bruno told them everything he knew about the matter, and after entreating them to find his daughter, he bade them good-bye

Step 1

Choose a specific and realistic goal

Noway Visits Benefico

Prince Noway rode to the marketplace and immediately began asking who was the wisest person around. Everyone he talked with said that Benefico was not only the wisest person around, but the most traveled one, too.

After getting directions from a farmer selling vegetables, he rode out the east road until he reached Benefico's house where he dismounted.

Feeling irritated because his first knock wasn't answered at once, he pounded impatiently on the door a second time. When Benefico opened it, Noway controlled his temper because he knew he needed the man's help.

"I am Prince Noway of Aber. I am here because I need your help to rescue Princess Melisande from Monstroso's Tower of Ice."

"I will be happy to help you," Benefico replied. "Are you sincere about this quest? It can be difficult, even dangerous. You may have to suffer certain hardships."

Hardships? Noway thought, the word taking some of the edge off his determination.

Finally, Benefico asked, "Are you really certain you want to do this?"

"Of course," Noway replied, not entirely honestly.

"Then let's begin," Benefico said. Matching his actions to his words, he unrolled a large map, placed it in front of Noway, and began to talk.

After half an hour, Noway's head was reeling. *I'll never remember all of this,* he thought. He looked at Benefico, who appeared ready to talk on indefinitely.

"Benefico, I don't have time for all of this talk. I think I'll start out and take my chances," he said, just before bolting through the door. Quickly untying his horse, he mounted and was gone in seconds.

Benefico looked after him in sorrow.

Kandu Visits Benefico

Although Kandu was eager to start his quest, he knew he had to have some help, so he walked to the marketplace in the center of town. He introduced himself to some of the people there and asked them who was the wisest person around. The answer was always, "Benefico."

"Where can I find him?" Kandu inquired.

"He lives just outside of town," a merchant told him. "Take the east road and follow it until you see a small, bright yellow house."

Kandu walked until he spied Benefico's house. At first he thought no one was home because despite his knocking, no one came to the door. "I can wait," he thought. "This is pretty important." Finally, he saw a figure approaching from behind the house.

"Who are you," the figure asked him, "and why are you bothering me?"

"My name is Kandu. I am determined to rescue the king's daughter from Monstroso, and I don't know how to begin. Everyone I talked to in the market said you were the wisest man around and suggested I come here. Will you help me?"

"Other men have made the same request of me, including one who was here earlier today.

I offered them help, but they were all too impatient to listen. Will you take the time to listen to me?" Benefico asked.

"I promise I will listen to every word. I am determined to find Princess Melisande and become her husband. I will do whatever I must to find her."

"Are you *really* sure you want to do this?" Benefico asked. "The journey may be long and it may be difficult, so you must be *absolutely* sure this is what you want to do. Are you?" he asked.

"Yes," Kandu said, "I have thought about this ever since I heard about the princess being stolen, and finding her is the most important thing in my life."

"Very well," the wise man replied. "I will help you as much as I can."

Step 2

Be determined to reach your goal.

Kandu Learns About His Journey

Benefico invited Kandu into his house. After offering him some refreshment, he brought out the map and pointed to a country marked, *The Country of Eternal Summer.*

"The country we now call Malfeaso was once the Country of Eternal Summer. When Monstroso took it over, ice and snow and blizzards appeared everywhere in it."

"You must pass through these countries to reach Malfeaso," the wise man said as he pointed to them on the map. "Each one is different from Giocoso and from each other. This is also true of those who live in them."

Benefico began telling him about each of the countries, what the people in them were like, and what he needed to know to pass through them.

When Kandu asked about Monstroso, Benefico told him that little was known of him, except that he was thought to be ruthless and would stop at nothing to achieve his ends.

Finally, Benefico said, "It's late. You are welcome to stay here tonight, and I will finish answering your questions in the morning."

Step 3

*Learn everything you can about what
you must do to achieve your goal*

Noway Begins His Journey

Prince Noway, having overheard a conversation between Kandu and a merchant, knew Kandu was not planning to leave for several days. *Good,* Noway thought, *I'll leave today and get a head start.* And so he did.

After riding for a few miles, he approached a farmer working near the road. "Do you know where the wizard Monstroso's tower is, my good man?" he asked.

"I'm not sure," the farmer replied, "but I think you have to go through Oberisk to get there. If not, I'm sure the king there could tell you."

"Thank you," Noway said, and rode on toward Oberisk at a leisurely pace.

He had left town in a hurry and he hadn't even thought about buying a map. As a result, he had to ask questions of people who knew even less than he did.

He diligently rode for the rest of the day, not with the bone-jarring speed that seemed to disagree with his digestion, but at a more comfortable pace.

Finally, seeing an inn up ahead, he stopped, rented a room, and then had a large dinner with plenty of the house wine. Tired from his exertions, he went upstairs and to bed, but not before berating himself for failing to bring a servant along.

Kandu Receives a Gift

The next morning Benefico answered more of Kandu's questions. A few hours later, the wise man said, "That is all I can tell you. But before you go, I have a gift for you."

He went over to a tall cabinet in a corner of the room, opened the door, and removed a small black object.

"This is a magical talisman," he explained. "As long as you carry it and keep your goal in mind, you will always be headed in the right direction. Look at it every day to remind yourself of the importance of what you're doing.

"You will be faced with many difficult decisions, and there will be temptations that can lure you away from your goal. Whenever you are uncertain or are tempted to give up, take out the talisman and it will help you make the right decision. If you are able to vanquish Monstroso, it will also bring you back here as soon as you wish."

"I am greatly in your debt, Benefico. How can I repay you?"

"You owe me nothing," Benefico said. "but, in the future when you are asked for aid, remember that someone once helped you freely without payment."

"Don't forget," the wise man said as they parted, "whenever you come to a fork in the road, *always* take the road to the right. If you follow your plan and my instructions you will get there quickly. If you do not follow them, you may never get there."

Noway Visits the Kingdom of Oberisk

After having a big breakfast the next day, Noway settled with the innkeeper and asked him for directions to Malfeaso and the Tower of Ice. The innkeeper seemed sure that Noway had to pass through Oberisk, so he pointed out the road which he thought led there.

Thus assured, Noway rode off. After just a few miles, he saw a sign that read, "The Kingdom of Oberisk." Once across the border, he rode steadily for a while and then stopped to rest at a fork in the road. As he rested, he heard hoof-beats, and turning, saw a small group of men approaching on horseback.

"Hello, Stranger. Where are you from, and where are you going?" one of the horsemen said.

Noway replied, "I am Prince Noway of Aber, and I am on a quest to find Princess Melisande and free her from the wicked wizard's Tower of Ice."

"Greetings, Noway, Prince of Aber. Welcome to the Kingdom of Oberisk. I am Prince Hubert. My father Ironicus is the king. We are having a banquet tonight, and you must be our guest."

"I'll gladly accept your invitation," Noway replied.

When they reached the castle, Noway dismounted and only minutes later was ushered into the presence of the king.

"Welcome to our kingdom," Ironicus said.

"Thank you, Your Majesty," Noway replied, with a courtly bow.

"I understand you wish to find the Tower of Ice," the king said.

"I do, indeed, Your Majesty."

"After you get settled in, you must join us at our banquet. Oberisk is renowned for its wines. You must try all of them while you're here."

"Thank you, Your Majesty," Noway replied.

He was shown to his room, where he bathed and changed clothing. Soon he was seated next to the king at the high table.

"I know you are on a quest," the king said, "and if you will stay with us for a few days, we'll try to find out exactly where the Tower is."

"I'd be happy to, Your Majesty. The princess has been in the tower for months already, so another day or so shouldn't matter."

Noway had such a pleasant time at the castle that he temporarily forgot about rescuing the princess. He had all he could eat and drink, someone to wait on him, and the company of attractive women. Four days passed before he remembered to ask the king about the Ice Tower.

"Your Majesty," he said when he next saw the king again, "were you able to find out the location of the Tower of Ice?"

"Not exactly," the king answered, "my astrologer said you must ride into the country of Well-Wishers and seek further directions there. It is but a day's journey from here. But you mustn't be in such a hurry to leave."

"Your Majesty, I must leave now, or I will never be able to find the princess." So, with great reluctance, Noway took his leave of Oberisk.

Kandu Makes Plans and Begins His Journey

From past experience, Kandu knew his most successful projects were those he had planned out carefully from the beginning. Since he was starting on the most important project he would ever undertake, he knew he must have a realistic plan to achieve it.

He went back to the market place and bought some parchment. He found a place to sit, took a charcoal stick from his pack, and began making notes. *This will be a long journey,* he thought, *but it won't seem so long if I break it down into a number of smaller journeys.*

He thought it would be best to consider each part of his journey as a separate goal. Then he made notes, so he could remember what Benefico had told him about each country and its inhabitants. Although it took him a little time to do this, he knew he would actually be gaining time by preparing for each country in advance.

Purchasing the supplies he needed, Kandu put them into his pack. His first small goal was to arrive at Giocoso's border by late afternoon. He knew he had reached it when he saw a sign ahead that said, "Well-Wishers."

He spied a haystack not far from the road, walked over to it, and sat down. Leaning back, he felt tired but relaxed. Opening his pack, he ate some bread and cheese and quickly fell asleep.

Step 4

Break your goal down into smaller goals and set a deadline for reaching each of them

Noway Visits The Country of Well-Wishers

It didn't take long to reach the country of Well-Wishers. Before Noway had gone far, he noticed a fork in the road. What had Benefico said? Was it the left or right road he should always take? *Which way shall I go?* he pondered

He looked toward the left-hand road and saw several people standing there. He rode over to them. "Hello," he said to the closest one. "Do you know where Monstroso's Ice Tower can be found?"

"I'm afraid not," the man replied, "but there will surely be someone here who does know."

"You know, you look kind of tired, like you could use a rest," one of the women said.

The prince was a bit of a hypochondriac, so he wasn't surprised that someone would say he didn't look well.

"I have a delicate constitution," he said, "and I do feel tired. Perhaps a short rest would be good for me. Is there an inn nearby?"

"Oh, yes, don't wear yourself out," another man spoke. "Just take the road in front of us, and you'll find one in a few miles."

The road was not a particularly good one, and Noway tried to hurry his horse whenever he saw some of the rather nasty-looking animals by its side. He rode on for quite some time before he saw an inn. It had an odd name: The Maldumer Inn. Dismounting, he went in and arranged for a room for the night.

Once inside, he noticed the inn was a little dirty and shabby and definitely not the kind of place he'd ordinarily have chosen. *Oh, well,* he thought, *it's better than sleeping outdoors.*

He spent a restless night in the inn. The people in the common room were quite noisy, and he had a little too much to drink with his dinner. When he awoke, he felt terrible but got out of bed and went downstairs.

The owner took one look at at him and said, "You still look tired. You don't want to wear yourself out, you know. Your health is more important than your quest. You should stay for a few more days."

Maybe I should, Noway thought, and went back to bed.

Three days later, having obtained directions from the innkeeper, he left the inn and rode until he saw a sign reading "Welcome to The Country of Attitude." Since there was no lodging in sight, he slept on the ground near the road, using his saddlebags for a pillow.

Kandu Visits The Country of Well-Wishers

Waking early the next morning, Kandu looked at the talisman and noticed it seemed brighter than the day before. He refreshed himself at a nearby stream and then crossed the border into the country of Well-Wishers.

Soon he saw a small group of people walking toward him.

"Greetings," a man said to him. "Where are you bound?"

"I'm on my way to rescue Princess Melisande from Monstroso's Tower of Ice," Kandu answered.

"Isn't that a pretty big task you've set for yourself? We don't want you to harm yourself by working too much or taking on too many responsibilities," a woman said. "And aren't you hurrying too much? You could become ill, you know. Better be more careful and slow down. Take some time off."

"Are you strong enough to do it?" another woman inquired. "You look like you could use a good rest."

The man inquired, "Are you sure it's not too much for you? You know, we only want what's best for you."

Fortunately, Benefico had told him about the two kinds of people he would meet there. He said those on the left-hand road would try to get him to abandon his goal. He knew better than to take their warnings seriously.

"No, my goal isn't too big for me, and yes, I know I can do it," Kandu said politely. "I have an important job to do, and I can't waste any more time here."

A few minutes later he spied a fork in the road and, as Benefico had instructed, took the road on the right. He knew he would meet positive, supportive people there.

The highway before him was gently curving and lined with tall trees. Before he had gone very far, he saw some people coming toward him.

"Where are you going?" one of the men asked.

"I'm on my way to Monstroso's Tower of Ice to rescue Princess Melisande," Kandu replied.

"That sounds like a worthwhile goal," the other man said. "You'll find you can travel quite rapidly on this road; it is never crowded."

"We'll be happy to walk along with you to the border of the next country if you like," the first man said.

Kandu replied, "That would be wonderful. You will be pleasant company." And so they started off toward the border, talking amicably as they walked.

"We all hope you succeed in your quest," said the woman when they reached the border. And with that, they turned and walked back the way they had come while Kandu continued on his way.

Step 5

Refuse to be lured away from your goal

Noway in the Country of Attitude

As a result of sleeping on the ground, Noway awoke feeling stiff and sore the next morning. This immediately put him in a foul mood.

He entered the country of Attitude and rode until he came to a fork in the road. "Which road should I take?" he asked himself. He flipped a coin, which, since it landed with the head up, meant he should take the left-hand road.

As he turned to go to the left, he saw three people approaching him on foot. They wore drab, colorless clothing. The man seemed depressed, one of the women was crying, and the other woman looked as though she was in terrible pain. "Where are you going in such a hurry?" the man asked.

"I'm on a quest to Monstroso's Tower of Ice, to rescue Princess Melisande," Noway said.

"It won't do any good, you know. Someone has probably rescued her already," the man responded. "It's probably too late."

"It's too dangerous to go there," one of the women said.

The pained-looking woman added, " You'll never be able to do it. It's impossible. Give up now. Don't waste any more of your time."

"Well, I'm not giving up!" Noway said defiantly and rode past them.

During the next few hours on the road he encountered many more people. Those who spoke with him tried to assure him his quest was hopeless. At first he ignored their comments, but then he began wondering if they were right. *Was he just wasting his time? Was there any point in going on? Had Melisande already been rescued?*

He realized that his chances of finding her were pretty poor. Since he'd left in such a hurry and hadn't listened to Benefico, he really didn't know where he was going or what to expect.

The longer he thought like this, the worse he felt. Finally, he decided to give up and turn back tomorrow. *How disappointing it is to have to retrace my steps, he thought.* Feeling somewhat depressed, he looked for some place to stay and finally came across a building with a sign that read, "Whycome Inn." After arranging for a room, he ate the tasteless meal set before him and then went upstairs to lie down on the lumpy bed he'd expected.

When he awoke the next morning, he felt dejected and even more depressed than the day before. He sighed pitifully as he got out of bed. He felt exhausted. This quest had really tired him out. "I will take better care of myself in the future," he promised himself.

After dressing and eating a dubious-looking gruel with mysterious lumps in it, he paid the innkeeper, had his horse saddled, and started back. As he rode, he kept running into people who said things like, "It's probably for the best," or, "You made a wise decision," or, "You'll be glad that you turned back."

Step 6

*Don't let anyone persuade you
to abandon your goal*

Kandu in the Country
of Attitude

Kandu awoke the next day feeling rested and relaxed. Looking across the border he saw a sign which read "You are entering the country of Attitude."

He took the talisman out of his pocket and, once again, the stone looked brighter than it had the day before. He ate a small meal and resumed his journey.

Soon he approached a fork in the road. Remembering Benefico's admonition to take the road on the right, he nonetheless paused and looked down the road to the left. It wound through swampy-looking country filled with dead trees. A little farther down the road he noticed three people coming his way. They wore ill-fitting, gray clothing and all looked quite unhappy.

"Where are you going?" the first man asked.

"I'm on my way to Monstroso's tower to rescue Princess Melisande," Kandu replied.

"You don't want to do this," The first man said.

"It won't work," the second man remarked.

The unpleasant woman added, "You'll never be able to do it. It's impossible. Give it up now, and you won't waste any more time."

"Well," Kandu said, "you may believe that, but I don't."

Hearing that, the trio turned and began walking back from where they had come.

People like this made it even easier for Kandu to remember Benefico's parting words, "When the road forks, *always take the road to the right*. If you do this, you will be able to pass through the country safely and quickly."

Kandu resumed walking, taking the road to the right. Before long he saw a small group of people approaching. Colorfully dressed, they were all smiling and looked happy.

"Where are you going, Traveler?" one of them asked.

"I'm on my way to Monstroso's tower to rescue Princess Melisande," Kandu replied.

"You know, if you really want to do it, you can," a tall man put in. "Once you've made up your mind to do it, you will."

The pleasant-looking woman added, "If you've got the strength of mind and determination, it's as good as done."

These people were much more to Kandu's liking! They were supportive and encouraging.

"I met some of the Negatives earlier and they tried to discourage me from going on," he said.

"You were right to avoid them," the tall man spoke. "No matter what anyone wants to do, they say it can't be done. They can make the happiest occasion seem dismal. They're against everything positive."

"We're the Positives," the man announced. "We remind you that you *can do* what you've set out to do. If you want to accomplish your goal, it's important to associate with Positives and avoid the Negatives."

"Thank you for your support and encouragement," Kandu told them. "I hope I'll see you again."

Kandu crossed the border into the next country. Since it was getting dark, he decided to stop there for the night. Tired, but hungry, he opened his pack and took some bread and cheese from his supplies. And having eaten, he opened his bedroll, lay down, and promptly fell asleep.

Step 7

Maintain a positive attitude

Noway Returns to the Country of Well-Wishers

Although the road seemed to go on forever, Noway finally reached the border between Attitude and Well-Wishers.

He crossed over and followed the same dismal road he had ridden before. Since he had not passed any other inn, he returned to the disreputable-looking inn where he'd stayed earlier. The owner greeted him. After Noway told him he'd given up his quest, the innkeeper said it was probably for the best anyway. "You don't want to wear yourself out, after all," he said. "Let somebody else do the hard work. Stay here for a few days and relax."

Several days later, Noway resumed his travel, riding slowly and lamenting his bad luck. "I guess I just wasn't meant to find her," he said to himself.

Kandu Enters The Country of Involvement

When Kandu awoke the next morning, he glanced up and saw a sign that said, "Involvement." He knew this was the country he must cross next.

He took out the talisman and looked at it again, as Benefico had suggested. It was glowing even brighter than it was yesterday. He smiled as he put it away in his pocket. Hungry once again, he quickly ate some bread and cheese from his pack, and then resumed his walk, eating pears and oranges he picked from trees growing near the road.

Before long he caught up with a man walking in front of him. "Good morning," Kandu said, "are you going very far?"

The man looked at him, shrugged his shoulders, and said, "I don't know."

"Don't you know where you're going?" Kandu asked him.

"No," the man said, "As far as I'm concerned, one place is pretty much the same as another."

He must be one of the Aimless that Benefico told me about, Kandu thought. *He said they are a sad people. They wander through life, not knowing or caring what happens to them.*

A few minutes later he saw a man and woman sitting on the grass on the left side of the road. Since their faces showed no hint of emotion, he knew they must be Aimless, too.

"Good morning," he said to them. "I'm on a quest to rescue Princess Melisande from Monstroso's Tower of Ice ."

"It won't make any difference," the woman replied. "What's the use?"

"Who cares, anyway?" the man said.

"I care," Kandu said, "because I am doing something that will make a big difference to many people," and he walked past them.

Just ahead he saw a fork in the road and again, as he had been told, took the road on the right. As he followed the gently curving road, he saw people on horseback coming toward him. He could tell by their laughter and smiles that they were the Motivated.

"Greetings, friend," one of the men called. "Where are you bound?"

"I'm on my way to Monstroso's Ice Tower to rescue Princess Melisande," Kandu answered. "You are the Motivated, aren't you?" Kandu asked.

"Yes," one of the group answered, "we know there are many important things to do, and we spend our lives doing and enjoying them."

"Your task is an important one, and we wish you great success," a young woman added.

"Thank you," Kandu said. "May you have a pleasant journey."

He walked until it began to get dark. *Where should I spend the night?* he wondered. Seeing a grove of trees close to the road, he decided to make a bed of pine branches and moss and sleep among the trees.

Tired from his long walk, he ate a small meal, curled up on his makeshift bed, and went to sleep. Tomorrow he would enter the country of Progress.

Step 8

Associate with other motivated people

Kandu Crosses The Country of Progress

As soon as Kandu awoke, he looked at his talisman. Once again, it was brighter than it had been the day before.

What at first looked like a lump of coal, now looked like a precious gemstone. Hurriedly, he refreshed himself at a nearby lake, ate a small breakfast, and crossed the border into Progress.

Thanks to Benefico, he already knew the kind of people he would find here. He started walking and soon saw a man and two women sitting on a bench near the side of the road. When he reached them, he told them who he was and that he was on a journey to Malfeaso to rescue Princess Melisande.

"Why do you want to do that?" the man asked. "What's wrong with just leaving things as they are? Why do you want to change them? Why don't you leave well enough alone?"

Kandu asked one of the women, "Don't you think it's best to try to make your lives better? Shouldn't you be working to improve things instead of just sitting there?"

"Why should we?" the woman asked. "Things are as fine as they can be. Why try to make them different?"

Kandu knew immediately that these people were some of the Statusquotians, a peculiar people who wanted things to always stay as they are. He replied, "There are often many good reasons to make changes." Sighing at their helpless outlook, he walked on.

A few miles after he took the right-hand road at the last fork, he saw a group of people walking in the same direction he was going. Even before he caught up with them, he knew they must be *Progressives,* because they all carried tools.

Kandu introduced himself and was greeted with smiles and warm handshakes. The workers were on their way to the border of Progress to repair some damage to a house that had once been occupied by Statusquotians. Apparently, the Statusquotians and the Progressives had once lived together, but the Statusquotians had moved away because they couldn't keep the Progressives from improving things.

Kandu said, "I'm on my way to Malfeaso to rescue Princess Melisande."

"That's certainly a situation that needs improving," one of the men replied. "Since we're going in the same direction as you, we'd be happy to walk with you for awhile."

"That's very kind of you," Kandu said, and they set off walking together.

Before long, the workers reached their destination and Kandu parted from them. But as he continued walking, he kept meeting people who cheered him on by saying things such as, "Keep up the good work, and you'll achieve your goal."

Step 9

*Until you have achieved your goal,
continue to concentrate on it*

Kandu Enters the Country of Uncertainty

As soon as Kandu awoke the next morning, he took the talisman out of his pocket to look at it. It was even brighter than it had been the day before and was glowing with a strong, steady light. "The closer I get to my goal, the brighter the talisman becomes," he observed.

He had stopped near the border the previous evening, and after refreshing himself and eating bread and cheese with some sweet-tasting fruit he had found, he crossed the border to the country of Uncertainty. He remembered what Benefico had told him about the people here: the citizens of Uncertainty are never quite sure what to do, so they do nothing.

After he had walked a short while, he noticed many people ahead of him on the road. They all seemed to be going in the same direction that he was. Walking up to a farmer, he asked, "Where is everyone going? What has happened?"

"None of us have gone into Malfeaso since Monstroso took it over. We are all on our way to the border, to see if more of the ice and snow have melted."

The woman with him said, "We are afraid of Monstroso, of course, and we've been afraid to go through the ice and snow the wizard brought with him. We're not certain it's safe."

"Beginning four days ago," the man added, "Malfeaso began to change. Starting at the border, the ice and snow began to melt. Each day it has receded a little more. If it continues like this, in a week or so it will probably all be gone. But even if it is, we're still afraid to go there because we're not certain if Monstroso is still there."

They were at the border by this time, and Kandu said, "Well, *I* am certain I must go into Malfeaso because I am determined to rescue Princess Melisande." And with that, he crossed the border into dread Malfeaso, leaving the Uncertains behind him.

Rescuing the Princess

Looking at his talisman again, Kandu started forward. He kept searching the horizon for the Tower of Ice, and although the country was flat enough for him to see for miles, he saw nothing that could be described as a tower.

As he continued walking, the ice and snow receded before him, and rich, green grass appeared, dotted with beautiful flowers of every description. Kandu heard birds singing joyously in the trees, and looking up, he saw the sky had changed from gray to brilliant blue. Warm breezes caressed his skin.

Although he still couldn't see a tower, a short way ahead he saw a small structure that appeared to be made of glass. The closer he got to it, the more insubstantial it became until finally it disappeared altogether.

He saw someone standing where the building had appeared to be and knew it must be Princess Melisande. Even from a distance he could tell that she was the most beautiful woman he had ever seen.

"I am Kandu. I have come to rescue you from the wizard, Your Highness," he said to her.

"You are my hero!" Melisande exclaimed. "I am *so* glad to see you. I thought I would *never* be rescued."

"But where is Monstroso?" Kandu asked, looking all around.

"When he saw you coming, he began running. That must be him way up the road," she said, indicating a rapidly diminishing figure in the distance.

"Oh, I can hardly wait to go home," the princess exclaimed. "I have been here for so long, and I have missed my family and my beautiful Giocoso."

"You won't have to wait at all, Princess, because I have a talisman that will take us there immediately."

He reached into his pocket for the talisman. When he pulled it out, it was warm to the touch and glowed so brightly is seemed as though a fire was blazing inside it. Kandu said, "Benefico told me that when I reached my goal, I did not have to retrace my steps."

Taking Melisande by the hand, he said the words that Benefico told him to use, "Talisman, take us to Giocoso," and instantly, they were there.

The Return to Giocoso

Needless to say, King Bruno was supremely happy when he learned that Princess Melisande and Kandu had arrived at the castle. After excitedly greeting them, he sent a messenger to fetch Benefico.

"Pardon me for taking so long to get here," the wise man said when he arrived. "The streets are filled with people rejoicing because their princess is back."

When they were all seated, Kandu told them about his journey.

"But why," King Bruno asked, "did he ask for money if he was such a great wizard? Why didn't he just use his wizardly powers to make some?"

"Because," Your Majesty, "Monstroso wasn't a wizard at all, just an ordinary person who was a master of illusions. He wanted money because all he could make was illusory money, and people soon notice it isn't real."

"The ice and snow of Malfeaso never existed," Kandu said, "They only seemed to because of his illusions. The country never changed. He also created the illusion of the Tower of Ice and did it so well that even Princess Melisande believed it was real. He thought he was safe because no one would dare to challenge his illusions."

"You were very brave to rescue my daughter, since there were so many obstacles in the way," King Bruno said.

"It's kind of you to say that, Your Majesty, but anyone else who took the same steps that I did could have done it," Kandu replied.

"It may be true that anyone *could* have done it, Kandu, but you actually *did* it," the king said. "And you, my dear," he said, addressing his daughter, "should begin planning your wedding immediately."

And how did everyone concerned feel about the way matters turned out? Kandu, needless to say, was happy that he would be marrying Princess Melisande. The princess, upon hearing the king had promised her hand to her rescuer, was delighted. Not only was Kandu handsome, he was also intelligent, and he had been willing to risk his life to save her. When she compared him with the other suitors who had courted her, she knew she could find no better man to marry, so marry they did.

Finally, when the royal wedding and all the festivities were over and King Bruno had a moment to be by himself, he smiled. He was quite pleased. His daughter, whom he loved very dearly, had been returned to him. And by rescuing the princess, his new son-in-law proved himself to be resourceful, smart, and brave. Having settled matters thus in his own mind, he knew that when he could no longer rule, he would leave the Kingdom of Giocoso in good hands.

Step 10

*Celebrate your success when
you achieve a goal*

Noway Returns to Oberisk

And what happened to Prince Noway? Since he'd given up the idea of rescuing Melisande, he was in no hurry to get back. He decided to go to Oberisk and stay with the king and prince once again, hoping to have as pleasant a time as he had earlier.

As he neared the castle, he saw a large party of nobles approaching from the opposite direction. He hurried to meet them, wondering what kind of occasion had prompted them to leave Oberisk.

When he asked where they had been, he learned they were returning from Giocoso. "We have just come back from Giocoso. We went there to attend the royal wedding," a woman told him.

"Royal wedding?" he said. "Who got married?" Noway asked her.

"Princess Melisande married the man who rescued her from the Tower of Ice," she answered. "It's a true love match, they say."

"Oh," Noway said. "Who was the groom?"

"His name is Kandu, and he comes from Schnell. Of course, it's *Prince* Kandu now," she added.

"Kandu?" Noway said. "How could he possibly have gotten there, freed the princess, come back and been married already?" the prince asked, thinking, *I should have been the one to rescue her. I had such great plans. He's just a commoner, while I am a prince.*

Although he had looked forward to enjoying the hospitality of the Oberiskian Court, Noway decided that, for the present at least, it might be best to return home to Aber and explain to his father what had gone wrong.

So Noway went on his way, not in any particular hurry, complaining about the injustice of it all, about how unfair life was, about how he deserved better, and so on until even his horse was tired of hearing about it.

The Class
Reunion

Part 2

After Bill completed the story, he went on. "My dad was a good father," he told Alan, "but he never made a lot of money. He didn't have much education, so he usually had to take what we call 'dead end jobs.' My mom had to watch every penny. I knew I wanted more out of life than he had been able to provide.

"You know, many people have never given serious thought to what they want, except in very general terms. And as the saying goes, if you don't know where you're going, you may end up anywhere. I knew I wanted a happy life, but specifically, I wanted a successful business, a happy marriage, and a happy home. After hearing Fred's story, I knew exactly how to go about getting them.

"Since I had made owning a successful business my highest priority, I went to work on it first. I broke that goal down into a series of smaller goals and broke some of them down even further. I made a check list of all of them so I could mark them off when I had achieved them."

"What did you do first?" Alan asked.

"I got a job with the city utility company," Bill replied. "I had to make a living while I was pursuing my goal. So, I worked for the city during the day, which left my nights free. One of my small goals was to learn something about business in general, before starting my own business. To accomplish this, I took some college business classes. In between college classes I worked on developing my products."

"What were those?" Alan asked.

"Since my mother had to work quite a bit, I ended up doing most of the cooking," Bill replied. "I became pretty good at creating my own sauces and gravies. I decided that I could parlay that talent into my own line of gravies and sauces, and I did. My company now makes all kinds of food products that are shipped all over the world.

"I won't bore you with all the details, but I went on pursuing my goals, one by one, until finally my company went public, and I was elected chairman of the board.

"During this time I met and fell in love with the wonderful woman I'm now happily married to. I'm just sorry she couldn't be here with us tonight.

"That's quite a story," Alan said. "It looks like your work and planning really paid off. Unfortunately, I'm too old to try to start a business."

"Too old! There are plenty of people much older than you who start businesses. Anyway, you don't have to start a business. You can follow these same steps to accomplish anything that will make an improvement in your life, like getting a better-paying job," Bill responded.

"You know," Alan said, with a big smile, "as soon as I get home tonight, I'm going to create my own goal list. Bill, you don't know how much meeting you again has done for me. And you're right—that was a great story."

"Here's my business card," Bill said. "Give me a call in six months. I'd like to find out how you are doing on your goals."

"You can bet I will," Alan replied, giving Bill an enthusiastic handshake. "And you know, Bill, I think meeting you here tonight was that big break I've been waiting for."

The Ten Steps to Achieving Your Goals

Step 1

Choose a specific, realistic goal. Narrow the focus of your goal and be sure it is attainable.

Step 2

Be determined to reach your goal. Someone who is determined to achieve a particular goal usually does.

Step 3

Learn everything you can about what you must do to achieve your goal. By doing this, you prepare yourself for what is to come.

Step 4

Break your goal down into smaller goals and set a deadline for reaching each one. A series of small goals seems much easier to achieve than one large one.

Step 5

Refuse to be lured away from your goal. Some people, often with the best of intentions, may try to convince you that you're spending too much time working toward your goal.

Step 6

Don't let anyone persuade you to abandon your goal. People who don't pursue goals themselves will encourage you to forget about yours.

Step 7

Maintain a positive attitude. You will find that a can-do attitude is a great help in achieving your goal.

Step 8

Associate with other motivated people. People who are trying to reach goals of their own will probably be the best companions for you.

Step 9

Until you have achieved it, continue to concentrate on your goal. The more you think about your goal, the closer you are to reaching it.

Step 10

Celebrate your successes as you achieve your goals. Make them special and enjoyable occasions.

Why the Ten Steps Work

Many of us seem to live in a continuous state of frustration. We feel unfulfilled because we can't get what we want or do what we want to do. This is a problem you can almost always fix, and since you can, why not do it?

If you haven't achieved your goals, it's probably for one or both of the following reasons:

> *First,* you have not chosen specific goals, only general ones, such as "I want to be

happy," or "I want a happy marriage," "I want a good job," or "I'd like to make a lot of money."

Second, if you *have* chosen specific goals, you have not created a plan of action to achieve them.

What happens when you don't have a plan? It's like setting out on a journey without a map and with a poor sense of direction; you could end up anywhere.

People who take the time to give thought to what they want and then prepare an organized action plan to achieve it, most often get what they want. Those who do not must accept whatever happens to them.

If you follow *The Ten Steps,* you will have an excellent chance of getting what you want. Give it a try, and you will prove it to yourself.

Acknowledgments

Once again I am indebted to Stacey Gilbert, Jean Names, Suzanne Sutherland, and Clif Bradley. Besides making always-helpful literary suggestions, they are wonderful friends of long standing. Thank you all for the contributions you have made to my books and to my life.

My thanks also to the Nova Development Corporation for the use of their graphic materials.

The Author

An accomplished musician, Jerry Minchinton performed professionally for a number of years before founding a mail-processing company. After guiding the firm through twelve years of steady growth, he withdrew from his executive position to devote more time to the study of self-esteem and related subjects.

Jerry graduated from Eastern Washington University with Highest Honors, received a Master of Arts degree from the same institution, and continued his education with doctoral studies at Florida State University.

A native of Wisconsin and a long-time resident of the Pacific Northwest, Jerry now lives and works in the beautiful Ozark Mountains of southern Missouri. His books have been translated into many languages and are sold throughout the world. He is a member of American MENSA.

Most people who have poor self-esteem don't know it!

If you...

- get your feelings hurt easily
- often feel guilty, angry or unhappy
- become upset when you're criticized
- feel uncomfortable if people don't like you
- find it hard to say "no"
- have painful feelings of unworthiness

...then you have experienced low self-esteem.

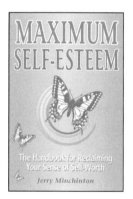

Poor self-esteem occurs as a result of accepting certain incorrect core beliefs as children. *Maximum Self-Esteem* identifies and explores these commonly-held but false beliefs. It reveals why gaining healthy self-esteem is not a matter of learning to like yourself better, but of learning to not dislike yourself.

Using effective methods and techniques, powerful affirmations and exercises, and self-scoring tests to measure your progress, this handy, practical guide makes good self-esteem accessible to everyone. *Maximum Self-Esteem* can radically transform your entire life, starting today!

Are you as happy as you want to be?

Most people aren't, because they lack the feelings of self-worth that are necessary to enjoy personal happiness.

To make good self-esteem easily accessible, Jerry Minchinton has distilled the basics into 52 valuable ideas, each of which can make a major contribution to the quality of your life.

In this book you will discover how to:

- boost your self-confidence
- develop more satisfying relationships
- ease emotional pain
- improve your outlook on life, and
- increase your happiness

Whether you want to make major improvements to your self-esteem or just add a little polish, you'll find this user-friendly book is perfect.

Why postpone happiness any longer? Read *52 Things You Can Do to Raise Your Self-esteem* and start enjoying life more today!

This is a book about problems —
YOUR problems

There are three levels from which you can approach your problems:

- Level 1 approaches work only by accident
- Level 2 approaches work occasionally
- Level 3 solutions almost always work

And which of these Levels do most of us use? The two least likely to work!

Using scenarios with multiple choices responses, *Wising Up* addresses the values, beliefs, and expectations that are at the heart of your problems. You'll find out how to:

- identify your problem-solving level
- avoid setting yourself up for problems
- solve problems quickly and effectively
- eliminate many problems permanently
- prevent problems before they start
- think about old problems in more helpful ways

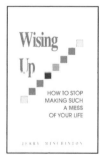

As you improve your problem-solving skills, you'll enjoy greater self-confidence and experience a new feeling of control over your life. If you would like a major improvement in your life, you'll find *Wising Up* is a powerful tool for change

What do you think?

We begin absorbing beliefs as children and add to them as long as we live. Most of the ideas we've locked into our belief system produce positive results, but some actually work *against* us. And since we are creatures of habit, we tend to go on thinking the same things we've *been* thinking, no matter how bad their effect on us.

Here are some examples.:

- I am unimportant and insignificant
- If I am rejected it's because there's something wrong with me
- I can't help being shy
- I always have terrible luck
- I'm awful because I sometimes hurt people's feelings
- I seem doomed to unhappy relationships
- My plans never seem to work out

The keys in this book can help you unlock these defective ideas and replace them with beliefs that work *for* you. Not only will you think better, you'll feel better and live better too!

Getting What You Want is a story within a story, a fable that teaches an important lesson. It is the heartwarming tale of Bill and Alan, friends who meet at a class reunion fifteen years after they graduated from high school.

Bill has made his dreams come true and achieved great things. Alan, unfortunately, has not. The secret to Bill's success lies in a story told to him by a very successful neighbor. The story shows you the **Ten Steps to Reaching Your Goals,** the steps you must take to turn your desires into reality and your hopes into achievements.

Getting What You Want offers the reader motivation, instruction, and an engrossing tale.

Here's the secret to getting what you want from life!

For additional copies of this book and other books by Jerry Minchinton, contact your local bookstore or order directly from the publisher.

ORDER FORM

Phone: Call 888-709-2559.
Fax: 417-261-2559
Money order or check: mail to: *Arnford House,*
     Route 1 Box 270, Vanzant MO 65768-9702
E-mail: arnford@townsqr.com

Please send:

_____ copies of *52 Things You Can Do to Raise Your*

     Self-Esteem   @ $7.95 each $_____

_____ copies of *Thinking Better*   @ $7.95 each $_____

_____ copies of *Maximum Self-Esteem*   @ $14.95 each $_____

_____ copies of *Wising Up*   @ $14.50 each $_____

_____ copies of *Getting What You Want* @ $8.95 each $_____

                           TOTAL $_____

Shipping: Continental U.S. add $2.95 for the
first book, $1 for each additional book to the
same address. Foreign: add $9 per book $_____

Missouri residents please add 6.25% sales TAX $_____

           TOTAL ENCLOSED $_____

Please allow 4 to 6 weeks for shipping

Name _____

Address _____

City & State _____

Zip Code _____

PAYMENT: ❏ Check   ❏ Money Order

Prices subject to change without notice